W9-BUG-496

DRA
Non fiction

Drawings Mondays, Wednesdays & Saturdays

The Science of Living Things

# What is a Marine Mammal?

# Bobbie Kalman & Jacqueline Langille

 Crabtree Publishing Company

# The Science of Living Things Series
## A Bobbie Kalman Book

**To Kevin,
with hugs from Heo**

**Editor-in-Chief**
Bobbie Kalman

**Writing team**
Bobbie Kalman
Jacqueline Langille

**Managing editor**
Lynda Hale

**Project editor**
Heather Levigne

**Editors**
Kate Calder
Jane Lewis
Hannelore Sotzek

**Computer design**
Lynda Hale
Campbell Creative Services (cover type)

**Photo research**
Hannelore Sotzek

**Consultant**
Erin Blackwood, M.Ed., Marine Science
Instructor, The Marine Mammal Center,
Sausalito, California

**Special thanks to**
Cynthia D'Vincent, Intersea Foundation; Kina Scudi, SeaWorld
San Diego

**Photographs**
Frank S. Balthis: front cover (elephant seals), pages 8, 11 (top), 12,
  19 (top), 30 (top)
Tom Campbell: pages 11 (bottom), 20 (bottom), 25
Cynthia D'Vincent: pages 14, 15, 31
Doc White/EarthWater: pages 9 (bottom), 20 (top)
Bobbie Kalman: pages 29, 30 (bottom)
Doug Perrine: page 16
Sea World, Inc./Bobbie Kalman: back cover (inset), page 26 (bottom)
Tom Stack & Associates: Mike Bacon: page 6; W. Perry Conway:
  page 26 (top); David Fleetham: page 24; Jeff Foott: pages 7 (bottom),
  13, 23; Barbara Gerlach: title page; Thomas Kitchin: pages 3, 9 (top),
  21; Randy Morse: pages 19 (bottom), 28; Michael S. Nolan: page 17
Other images by Digital Stock and Eyewire, Inc.

**Illustrations**
Barbara Bedell: pages 4-5, 14, 15, 17, 18 (middle, bottom),
  22, 29 (middle)
© Crabtree Publishing Company: pages 12, 27 (top), 29 (bottom)
Barb Hinterhoeller: page 27 (bottom)
Jeannette McNaughton-Julich: page 8
Trevor Morgan: page 18 (top)

## Crabtree Publishing Company

PMB 16A
350 Fifth Avenue,
Suite 3308
New York, NY
10118

360 York Road,
RR 4
Niagara-on-the-Lake,
Ontario, Canada
L0S 1J0

73 Lime Walk
Headington,
Oxford
OX3 7AD
United Kingdom

**Cataloging in Publication Data**
Kalman, Bobbie
   What is a marine mammal?

(The science of living things)
Includes index.

ISBN 0-86505-936-5 (library bound)  ISBN 0-86505-954-3 (pbk.)
This book describes the ways in which marine mammals have adapted to
ocean habitats, including physiology, reproduction, diet, and other behavior.
1. Marine mammals—Juvenile literature. [1. Marine mammals.] I. Langille,
Jacqueline. II. Title. III. Series: Kalman, Bobbie. Science of living things.

QL713.2.K35 2000                          j599.5                          LC 99-23814
                                                                           CIP

# Contents

# What is a marine mammal?

A **mammal** is an animal that drinks milk from its mother's body as a baby. All mammals are **warm-blooded**, which means their body temperature stays the same in warm or cold places. Most mammals have some hair or fur on their body. About 4600 **species**, or types, of mammals live on Earth.

**Marine mammals** are mammals that have **adapted**, or become suited to, living in salt water. They spend much of their time in the ocean and depend on the sea for food. There are 140 species of marine mammals including whales, seals, walruses, sea lions, sea otters, manatees, dugongs, and polar bears.

*dugong*

*Manatees and dugongs make up the* **sirenian** *group. All sirenians live in salt water except one manatee species that lives in rivers.*

baleen whale

toothed whales

*harbor porpoise*

*common dolphin*

*humpback whale*

*Whales, dolphins, and porpoises are* **cetaceans**. *Cetaceans spend their entire life in water. Whales are divided into two groups—**toothed whales** and **baleen whales**.*

*beaked whale*

4

# Land and sea

Some marine mammals do not spend their entire life in the ocean. Seals, sea lions, and walruses often leave the water and rest on land. Polar bears roam over ice floes in winter and live on shore during the summer. Sea otters rest on land during storms. Although these animals spend time out of the ocean, they belong to the marine mammal group because they depend on the sea for food.

*sea lion*

*Seals, sea lions, and walruses belong to a group of marine mammals called **pinnipeds**. Members of this group have flattened flippers instead of paws or feet.*

*walrus*

*The sea otter belongs to the **mustelid** group, which also includes skunks and weasels. It is the only type of mustelid that is a marine mammal.*

*sea otter*

*polar bear*

*Like other marine mammals, the polar bear relies on the ocean for food. It spends much of its time in the cold ocean waters. A polar bear's thick layer of body fat and fur help keep it warm.*

# Life in the ocean

Scientists think that marine mammals **evolved**, or changed gradually, from animals that lived on land. Long ago, some land animals began hunting in or near oceans and spending less time on land. They learned to dive, hunt, and swim to survive. Over millions of years, their body adapted to life in the water, and the ocean became their home.

A marine mammal's body is **streamlined**, or sleek, to help it move easily through water. Some marine mammals have paddle-shaped limbs that they use to move their body through the water. Others use only their tail. All marine mammals have strong muscles for swimming. They are super swimmers!

# A breath of fresh air

Marine mammals swim, eat, and sleep in the ocean but cannot breathe underwater. Mammals breathe air through **lungs**. Lungs are organs inside an animal's body that take in and release air. Even marine mammals such as whales, manatees, and dugongs, which spend their entire life in water, need to come to the surface to breathe. Marine mammals dive underwater to search for food or escape from enemies. Before diving, they close their nostrils to keep out water.

*Dolphins have one **blowhole** on top of their head for breathing.*

# Staying warm

Marine mammals need to keep their body warm in their cold **habitat**, or home. Most have a thick layer of **blubber**, or fat, under their skin that helps **insulate** their body. Some also rely on a fur coat. Two types of hair help keep their body warm. A thick coat of **underfur** traps air near their body to keep the animal warm. An overcoat of long **guard hairs** protects the underfur when the animal dives underwater.

# Marine senses

Most animals use five senses to learn about their surroundings: hearing, sight, smell, taste, and touch. Marine mammals rely mainly on their senses of sight, touch, and hearing. Living in the water does not require a good sense of smell or taste.

## Good vibrations

Activity causes water to **vibrate**, or move quickly back and forth. Marine mammals have sensitive skin that allows them to feel vibrations in water. An animal that senses vibrations knows that food or an enemy is moving nearby.

## Echolocation

Some whales use **echolocation** to gather information about their surroundings. They make sounds underwater such as clicks or chirps, which make vibrations. The vibrations bounce off nearby objects and return to the whales as echoes. By listening to the echoes, whales can determine the size, distance, and location of objects in the water.

*Pinnipeds that spend time on land in large groups can be noisy. Some male pinnipeds roar to scare away other males.*

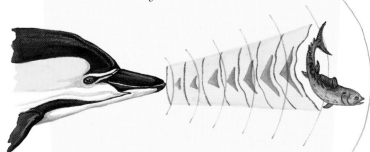

*Dolphins have no vocal cords. They do not open their mouth to make noises. Instead, the sounds they use when echolocating come from **nasal sacs** inside their head.*

## What a racket!

Many marine mammals make noises to **communicate**, or send messages to one another. Whales and dolphins make sounds that travel for miles underwater. On land, some species use sounds to identify members of their group. A mother seal can recognize her baby among hundreds of other babies by the sound of its cry.

## Big whiskers

A sense of touch is important for marine mammals that hunt for food at night or in deep water where there is little light. Marine mammals have long hairs called **whiskers** around their mouth to sense vibrations and objects in the water.

## Do you see what I see?

How well a marine mammal can see often depends on where it lives. Manatees, which have small eyes, live in shallow coastal areas. The plants they eat grow near the surface and are easy to see. Elephant seals, however, have good eyesight that helps them find food deep in their ocean home.

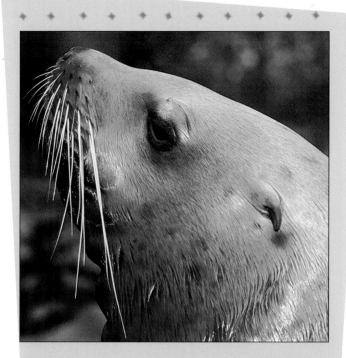

*This Steller sea lion uses its whiskers to feel the vibrations made by fish—its favorite food!*

*Seals dive deep to find food on the ocean floor. Their excellent eyesight helps them find food in the deepest, darkest part of their home.*

# Family life

In order to have babies, male and female marine mammals **mate**. A baby then grows inside the female's body. Mammals give birth to **live young**. Their young does not hatch from eggs. Most marine mammals give birth to only one baby after mating because it is difficult to take care of two babies at once. In most species, the mother feeds and protects her young without any help from the father.

*Female manatees, shown below, and dugongs do not have teats on their belly or chest as most mammals do. Instead, their baby feeds from teats behind each flipper.*

## Milk for the baby

Mammals **nurse** their baby, feeding it milk from their body. Milk is made inside a female's **mammary glands** and leaves her body through nipples or teats on her body. The baby nurses through a slit in the mother's belly. Marine mammal milk is high in fat and rich in vitamins, which babies need for growing.

## Caring mothers

Most marine mammals are active soon after they are born. Their mother protects them from predators and teaches them how to swim and hunt. Many seals, however, do not teach their baby these skills—the baby learns to survive on its own.

*(top) Many mothers nurse their baby for more than six months. This elephant seal is spilling some of its mother's milk. (bottom) A mother sea otter cradles her baby on her chest to keep it warm and dry.*

# A seafood feast

All animals need food for **energy**. Living in an **aquatic** habitat requires a lot of energy for swimming and keeping warm, so marine mammals must eat large amounts of food to survive. They eat food that lives in or near oceans. Some are **carnivores**, or meat-eaters. Others are **herbivores**, which means they eat mainly plants. Some marine mammals are **opportunistic feeders**. If their favorite food is not available, they eat whatever they can find.

Most marine mammals are **predators**—they hunt and eat animals. Many eat **krill** and other **crustaceans** such as shrimp and crabs. Marine mammals also eat **mollusks** such as squid, clams, snails, sea urchins, and sea stars. Seals, dolphins, whales, and sea lions eat fish.

*Elephant seals hunt penguins. When both animals are on land, the penguins are safe because the seal moves too slowly to catch them. In the water, however, the seal swims quickly beneath a penguin and catches it easily.*

## Getting water

All animals need a small amount of salt so their body will work properly. Most land animals get enough salt from the food they eat. If they drink salt water, they become sick. Marine mammals swallow salt water with their food, but it does not make them sick. Their body has adjusted to eating in the ocean.

## Storing food

When animals eat, some of the energy they get from their food is stored in their body as fat. The animal's body breaks down the fat at a later time when it needs the energy. For many marine mammals, the stored fat is also a source of water. If their body needs moisture, it breaks down some of the fat to make water.

*Manatees, shown above, and dugongs are the only marine mammals that are herbivores. They eat plants such as sea grass. Plants provide fewer nutrients than meat, so sirenians need to eat large amounts of food to get enough energy to survive. Some eat up to 100 pounds (45 kg) of food each day!*

# Baleen whales

The largest animals in the oceans are baleen whales. One species, the blue whale, may be the largest animal that has ever lived on Earth— even bigger than a dinosaur! Baleen whales often spend their summers in the cold waters around the North Pole, where krill are plentiful. After months of feeding, their blubber becomes very thick. Then the whales **migrate**, or travel, to warmer oceans in order to mate. At the breeding grounds, many species do not eat. They live off their body fat until they have mated and it is time to return to their feeding grounds once again.

*right whale*

*blue whale*

*Whales such as this humpback often **breach**, or leap into the air and land on their back or side, making a huge splash!*

## Feeding through a filter

Baleen whales have no teeth for grasping or chewing food. Instead, they filter food from the water through baleen. Baleen is made up of long plates of **keratin**—the same stiff material of which fingernails are made. The plates hang in the whale's mouth like the bristles of a broom. To feed, a baleen whale takes in a huge mouthful of water and food. It pushes out the water with its tongue, trapping fish, krill, and other tiny animals in the baleen, and then swallows its meal.

*krill*

*Humpback whales often feed in groups. They sing a high-pitched **feeding song** that stuns fish and causes them to stop swimming. While the fish are stunned, the humpbacks lunge upward and—GULP!*

# Toothed whales

Toothed whales make up the largest group of marine mammals. There are 66 species of toothed whales, including sperm whales, dolphins, porpoises, the narwhal, and the beluga. Some toothed whales only have two teeth, but others have as many as 70.

Most species of toothed whales are **social** animals, which means they live in groups. A group of whales that spends most of its time together is called a **pod**. A pod may be as small as one family with a few cousins, or it may consist of hundreds of whales.

## Big appetites

**Orcas** belong to the dolphin family. They are also called killer whales because they are great hunters. There are two types of orcas: **transients** and **residents**. Transient orcas travel from place to place, hunting for food. They eat mainly marine animals including porpoises, sea lions, and seals. Resident orcas live in one area in small groups and eat mainly fish such as sardines, salmon, and tuna.

## How do whales sleep?

To sleep in water, some whales float at the surface with the top of their head above water so they can breathe through their blowhole. This type of rest is called **logging**. Other whales rest underwater and rise to the surface every few minutes so they can breathe.

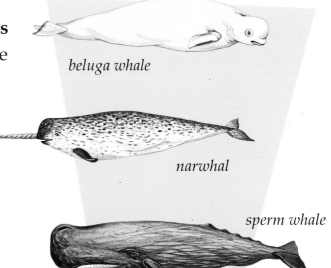

*beluga whale*

*narwhal*

*sperm whale*

*(top) Orcas have a large body and require a lot of energy for swimming. They need to eat a lot of food to survive. (above) Belugas and narwhals are closely related. The sperm whale is the largest of the toothed whales.*

# Pinnipeds

There are more than 30 species of pinnipeds. The pinniped family is divided into three groups: **crawling** seals, **walking** seals, and the walrus, which is the only species in its group. With flippers for feet, pinnipeds are excellent swimmers. The word pinniped means "fin-footed."

*Harp seals are crawling seals. They are named for the harp-shaped markings on their body.*

## On the seashore

Unlike whales, pinnipeds often come out of the water. They leave the water to rest, mate, give birth, and **molt**, or shed their old fur. On land, most pinnipeds spend time crowded together in large groups. Members of a certain group usually return to the same beach year after year.

*This Steller sea lion belongs to the walking seal group.*

## Family names

Pinnipeds and some other mammals are identified using special names. Adult males are called **bulls**. Adult females are called **cows**. In some pinniped species, one adult male has many female mates. His group of females is called a **harem**. Baby seals are called **pups** until they are about five months old, and then they are **yearlings**.

*The walrus has some traits of both crawling and walking seals, so it is in its own group.*

# Crawling seals

Crawling seals make up the largest group of pinnipeds. To move on land, they drag themselves by their front flippers or wiggle along the surface. In the water, however, crawling seals are fast, agile swimmers. They wag their back flippers from side to side to move through the water. Crawling seals are often called **earless** seals because they have no ear flaps. They do, however, have ear holes.

*This elephant seal has a mouthful of kelp, but it does not eat plants. It feeds mainly on fish.*

*Elephant seals use their flippers to throw sand onto their back when they are on land. The sand helps cool their body and prevent their skin from becoming sunburned.*

# Walking seals

*(above) This California sea lion is leaping out of the water.
(right) Walking seals have a longer, more flexible neck than that of crawling seals.*

Fur seals and sea lions are walking seals. On land, they turn their hind flippers forward and walk on all fours. In the water, they use their front flippers to swim. Unlike crawling seals, walking seals have small ear flaps.

## Lions of the sea

Sea lions were named after the lion because some male sea lions have a mane of thick hair around their neck that looks similar to a male lion's mane.

# Walruses

The walrus is one of the larger members of the pinniped family. It has some of the same features as both walking and crawling seals. Like crawling seals, walruses have ear holes instead of flaps. On land, walruses can turn their back flippers forward and walk on all fours as walking seals do. Walruses often **haul out** onto land, where they spend most of their time sleeping.

Both male and female walruses have two long, strong teeth called **tusks** that grow throughout the animal's life. The male walrus with the biggest tusks leads the **herd**, or group. Walruses use their tusks for protection against predators and for hauling out. They dig their tusks into an ice floe and pull their body out of the water. Males also use them to fight with other males during mating season.

*A large group of walruses is called a **colony**. Thousands of walruses may live in a single colony. They are peaceful unless they are attacked. An entire colony will come to the aid of a member that is in danger.*

# Sea otters

Sea otters live only along the northern portions of the Pacific Ocean. They stay close to shore, where the water is shallow. There, sea otters can easily dive to the ocean floor to find food. Beds of **kelp**, or seaweed, growing in the ocean provide protection for sea otters. When they are resting, they wrap themselves in the kelp to keep from floating out to sea. Kelp also helps camouflage these animals from predators such as orcas.

## Low-fat mammals

Sea otters are the only marine mammals that have no blubber. Instead, they have a thick fur coat to help keep their body warm. The inner layer of fur acts as a warm blanket. Long outer guard hairs help keep water away from the underfur and skin. Sea otters **groom**, or clean, their fur constantly. When the fur gets dirty, it sticks together in clumps, allowing the underfur and skin to become wet and cold.

*Sea otters must eat constantly to get energy to stay warm in cold waters. They also spend much of their time resting to save their energy. The only parts of a sea otter's body that are not covered in its protective fur are its ears, eyes, nose, paws, and flippers, which it holds in the air and out of the cold water.*

*The sea otter is one of the few types of animals that uses tools. It uses stones to pry shellfish off rocks on the ocean floor. To open the hard shells, it holds a rock on its stomach and pounds the shell on it until it cracks.*

# Sirenians

One dugong species and three species of manatees make up the sirenian group. Sirenians have a large, bulky body, two paddle-shaped forelimbs, and a thick, flat tail. They have no back legs. Although they have blubber under their skin, manatees and dugongs do not need it to keep warm—they live only in warm waters. The blubber is a source of stored food that sirenians need to survive during seasons when fewer plants grow in their habitat.

Manatees have four rows of flat teeth called **molars**. The sea grasses and plants that make up a manatee's diet contain hard, gritty bits of sand and **silica**. Chewing these hard materials gradually wears down the animal's teeth. As the teeth wear down, they slowly move forward in the manatee's jaw and eventually fall out. A new set of teeth then replaces the old set. The teeth of a manatee are replaced many times throughout its life.

## Slow movers

Sirenians **graze**, or move slowly as they munch on plants, just as cows do. Many people call them sea cows. Sirenians use their flat tail for swimming. They move too slowly, however, to get out of the way of motorboats. The boat propellers cut into the animals' back, leaving deep wounds or killing them. In shallow waters in Florida, there are signs warning boaters to be careful, but many manatees are still injured.

### Manatee or dugong?

**Manatee:**
- rounded tail
- plump body
- rough skin
- no tusks

**Dugong:**
- deep notch in tail
- streamlined body
- smooth skin
- males have tusks

Did you guess that the animal in the picture on the left is a dugong and the one below is a manatee?

# Polar bears

*Polar bears are strong swimmers. When they come out of the water, they shake their body and rub it on the snow to dry themselves.*

Polar bears are the largest members of the bear family, and they are the only bears that live in the Arctic. They are well adapted to hunting in their icy habitat. To catch a seal, a polar bear waits next to a hole in the ice. When a seal pops its head out of the water to take a breath, the polar bear grabs it.

## Thick, white fur

A polar bear's fur coat is made up of hollow hairs. Each hair directs the heat from the sun to the polar bear's skin. A polar bear's nose is black like the rest of its body. Dark skin helps absorb heat and keep the polar bear warm.

## Fantastic feet

A polar bear's feet are ideal for swimming and walking on ice. Their wide feet and webbed toes help them swim, and the long hair that grows between their foot pads helps keep them warm. The soles of a polar bear's feet have small bumps and hollows like suction cups that grip the ice, making it easy to walk on the slippery surface.

*Like many young animals, polar bear cubs often play, nipping each other and rolling in the snow.*

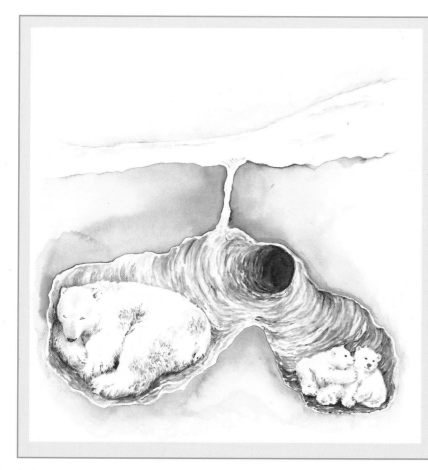

## Raising babies

Female polar bears usually give birth to twins. Newborn cubs rely on their mother for food and warmth, and they nurse every few hours. Their eyes stay closed for several weeks so they rely on their mother for protection. The cubs stay on land for several weeks in a den dug out of the snow, as shown left. When the cubs are three or four months old, they are ready to leave the den. The mother bear teaches her young how to hunt and swim. The cubs stay with their mother until they are two years old, and then they are able to go off on their own.

# Danger!

Most of the dangers that affect marine mammals are caused by people. For hundreds of years, people have hunted sea animals for their meat, oil, blubber, skin, and fur. Marine mammals also suffer from pollution, over-fishing, and collisions with boats. Many species are **endangered**, or in danger of dying out. Manatees, monk seals, Steller sea lions, and many species of baleen whales are endangered.

Oil spills, plastic trash, and poisons pollute the oceans around the world. Oil kills the food that marine mammals need to survive. Oil also sticks to fur, making it difficult to clean. Oily fur causes seals and sea otters to freeze to death. Some animals eat plastic, which makes them sick and often kills them.

*Seals get caught in fishing nets when they are small. As they grow, the nets tighten around their neck and cut into their skin.*

## Collisions

Whales and manatees often rest and sleep close to the water's surface. Sometimes they sleep so deeply that they do not notice boats coming near them or they do not wake up in time to get out of the way. When a boat hits an animal, it often dies from broken bones and deep cuts.

## The fisheries

People catch and sell many of the same types of fish and shellfish that marine mammals eat. In some areas, too much fishing by humans leaves little food for sea animals, causing them to starve. Dolphins, whales, and seals also get caught in fishing nets and drown.

## Helping marine mammals

In the past, people hunted and killed thousands of marine mammals. Today, many species are protected from hunters, but some people still hunt them illegally. Members of the **International Whaling Commission** help protect whales in their natural habitat. To learn more about helping whales and other marine mammals, you may contact organizations on the Internet, such as the **National Wildlife Federation** at www.nwf.org/nwf/ or the **World Wildlife Fund** at www.wwf.org.

*Monk seals are an endangered species in Hawaii.*

*Some marine mammals such as manatees have only one baby every two years, making it difficult for their numbers to increase.*

*Although it is illegal, some people kill walruses for their ivory tusks.*

# Marine mammals and people

*(above) This scientist is showing a young sea otter how a mother otter carries a baby on its chest.*
*(below) Dolphins like to be touched.*

Many types of marine animals live in marine **aquariums**, **seaquariums**, or **oceanariums**. Seaquariums and oceanariums are usually built on the ocean or in a bay or river. They also have outdoor pools with clear windows so that visitors can see the marine animals below the water's surface. Dolphins, porpoises, orcas, seals, sea lions, and sea otters are the marine mammals most often found in oceanariums.

## Studying marine mammals

Seaquariums allow scientists to study marine mammals up close. The scientists provide visitors with information about all kinds of marine life. Oceanariums also help people gain respect for the animals and teach them how to help marine animals survive in the wild.

## Rescuing injured animals

Many aquariums rescue injured marine mammals. The scientists at an oceanarium work hard to save an animal and bring it back to health. When it has recovered, they take it back to the ocean and set it free.

*(opposite) Most people do not get this close to a humpback whale, but these scientists are studying the whales so that people will learn more about these marine mammals.*

# Words to know

**aquatic** Describing something in or near water

**breach** The act of a whale leaping out of the water

**crustacean** An animal that has a hard shell and a jointed body and legs

**energy** The physical power needed for moving and breathing

**evolve** To change or develop slowly over time

**feeding song** A loud, high-pitched call used by humpback whales to herd their prey into a group

**guard hair** A long hair that protects an animal's underfur and keeps it from becoming waterlogged

**insulate** To cover with material that stops heat from entering or leaving the body

**keratin** The hard substance that forms baleen

**krill** A tiny animal that is eaten by baleen whales

**lungs** Organs used by animals to breathe oxygen from air

**mammary gland** An organ used by a female mammal to produce milk for her young

**mate** Joining together to make babies

**migrate** To move from one location to another in order to mate or find food

**mollusk** An animal that has a hard shell and a soft body

**mustelid** A mammal group that includes weasels and sea otters

**nasal sac** A hollow organ in a dolphin's snout that is used to produce sounds

**silica** A hard, odorless, colorless mineral

**underfur** The hairs that insulate a mammal's body

# Index

air  7, 14, 22
aquariums  30
babies  9, 10, 11, 18, 27, 29, 30
baleen  4, 14-15, 28
belugas  16, 17
blowhole  7, 17
blubber  7, 14, 20, 24, 28
blue whales  14
boats  25, 28, 29
body  4, 6, 7, 10, 11, 13, 14, 17, 18, 19, 21, 22, 24, 25, 26
breathing  7, 17, 26
cetaceans  4
dangers  21, 28-29
diving  6, 7, 9, 22
dolphins  4, 7, 8, 9, 12, 16, 17, 29 , 30
dugongs  4, 7, 10, 13, 24, 25
ears  19, 20, 21, 22
echolocation  8
enemies  7, 8
energy  12, 13, 17, 22
eyes  9, 22, 27
fat  7, 11, 13, 14, 22
feet  18, 25
fish  9, 12, 15, 17, 19, 29
fishing  28, 29

flippers  10, 18, 19, 20, 21, 22
food  5, 7, 8, 9, 12, 13, 15, 17, 22, 24, 27, 28, 29
fur  4, 5, 7, 18, 20, 22, 26, 28
habitat  7, 12, 24, 26, 29
hair  4, 7, 9, 20, 22, 26, 27
home  6, 7, 9
humpback whales  14, 15, 30
hunting  6, 8, 11, 12, 17, 26, 27, 28, 29
ice  5, 21, 26, 27
killer whales  see orcas
krill  12, 14, 15
land  5, 6, 8, 9, 11, 12, 13, 18, 19, 20, 21, 27
lungs  7
manatees  4, 7, 9, 10, 13, 14, 24, 25, 28, 29
mating  10, 14, 18, 21
milk  4, 11
mother  4, 9, 10, 11, 27, 30
mouth  8, 9, 15, 19
narwhals  16, 17
ocean  4, 5, 6-7, 9, 12, 13, 14, 20, 22, 23, 28, 30
orcas  17, 22, 30
penguins  12
people  25, 28, 29, 30

pinnipeds  5, 8, 18-21
plants  9, 12, 13, 19, 24, 25
polar bears  4, 5, 26-27
pollution  28
porpoises  4, 16, 17, 30
predators  11, 12, 21, 22
right whales  14
rivers  4, 30
scientists  6, 30
sea lions  4, 5, 9, 12, 17, 18, 20, 28, 30
seals  4, 5, 9, 11, 12, 17, 18, 19, 20, 21, 26, 28, 29, 30
sea otters  11, 22-23, 28, 30
senses  8-9
shellfish  23, 29
sirenians  4, 13, 24-25
skin  7, 8, 19, 22, 24, 25, 26, 28
sperm whales  16, 17
swimming  6, 7, 11, 12, 15, 17, 18, 19, 20, 25, 26, 27
tail  6, 24, 25
teeth  4, 12, 16, 17, 21, 24
tusks  21, 25, 29
walruses  4, 5, 18, 21, 29
whales  4, 7, 8, 9, 12, 14-17, 18, 28, 29, 30

1 2 3 4 5 6 7 8 9 0  Printed in the U.S.A.  8 7 6 5 4 3 2 1 0 9